God's Si♥

God's Si♥

Jose Maria Pereyra Jacinto

Copyright © 2025 by Jose Maria Pereyra Jacinto.

All rights reserved. No part of this publication may be reproduced, distributed, or transmitted in any form or by any means, including photocopying, recording, or other electronic or mechanical methods, without the prior written permission of the copyright owner and the publisher, except in the case of brief quotations embodied in critical reviews and certain other noncommercial uses permitted by copyright law. For permission requests, write to the publisher, addressed "Attention: Permissions Coordinator," at the address below.

ARPress
45 Dan Road Suite 5
Canton MA 02021

Hotline: 1(888) 821-0229
Fax: 1(508) 545-7580

Ordering Information:
Quantity sales. Special discounts are available on quantity purchases by corporations, associations, and others. For details, contact the publisher at the address above.

Printed in the United States of America.

ISBN-13:	Softcover	979-8-89676-111-2
	eBook	979-8-89676-112-9

Library of Congress Control Number: 2025901518

Table of Contents

Foreword vii
Prayer ix
Endorsement of God's SI xv
Unidentified Aerial Phenomenon (UAP)
      and Jesus Christ by a UFO Genie xvi
Regarding Spirituality Physics of God xxi
Chapter 1: Difference Between Dark Energy and Dark Matter 1
Chapter 2: Space and Time 4
Chapter 3: Harmonics of Bipolarity 5
Chapter 4: Real Intent of God 6
Chapter 5: Stuff of Space 8
Chapter 6: Differentiation of Energies 10
Chapter 7: Divine Organ 11
Chapter 8: Heavenly Boundaries 12
Chapter 9: The Biggest of the Big and the Smallest of the Small .. 14
Chapter 10: Universe Inside An Atom 16
Chapter 11: Spirits Of Matter 18
Chapter 12: Free Will (Man's Spirit) 19
Chapter 13: Magnificence of Nothing 21
Chapter 14: Infinity Web 23
Chapter 15: Why Man Is Imperfect 26
Chapter 16: Stuff Of God 28

Chapter 17: No Yin and Yang 29

Chapter 18: Intelligence As A Tool 31

Chapter 19: What Is Good or Bad? 33

Chapter 20: Atom As An Intelligent Entity 34

Chapter 21: God's Intelligence Is Different From Ours 35

Chapter 22: God's Superdense Kingdom 36

Chapter 23: Science of God's Love Energy 39

Chapter 24: Miracle Lifeline 41

Chapter 25: Nondestructive God Energy 42

Chapter 26: Seven Heavens Redefined 44

Chapter 27: No Other God Died For Us Here On Earth 45

Chapter 28: Why is The Soul Created 46

Chapter 29: Stuff Of The Mind...47

Chapter 30: Being Positive 49

Chapter 31: The Splendor of the Power of Love Energy 50

Chapter 32: Communication with God through Physics...........52

Chapter 33: Catholic Mystery: The Trinity 55

Chapter 34: Proof God has not been Created 58

FOREWORD

The essence of a Creator or God means He is not created since He is the creator of Himself. In God's world, there are no elements of time and space unlike in our universe where creation can prosper utilizing space and time.

God, the Father has sent His son, Jesus Christ, to save us from our sins exactly or at the utmost proper time. Humans who behave like animals with beast-like attitudes cannot think or exercise their puny minds to be able to choose good from bad or love from hate. In other words, they have no functional FREEWILL with the capacity to rationalize their significance. It is only now after 2000 years that we, humans, after CHRIST's exemplification, are only now waking up to be able appreciate the meaning of LOVE.

Man's freewill emanating from his soul, is stationed with god, the Father. Man's spirit (freewill) migrates to his mind located within the vicinity or magnetic field of his brain. It's function is to work to be able to earn and enjoy the fruits of God's love within His Kingdom. His freewill must satisfactorily choose love instead of hate and right from wrong.

Our creation by God ignited from the Big Bang dispersing time and space. Simultaneously, an Aka Cord is created facilitating communication between God and man and for God to answer the prayers of man.

He is truly our GOD

The contents of this work, including, but not limited to, the accuracy of events, people, and places depicted; opinions expressed; permission to use previously published materials included.

PRAYER

I beseech you O'Lord, my Master and Creator. I am not worthy enough to even glance at you. Yet, I dare step into your cloak and try to know the unknowable You. You do not play dice. Only a God can create a universe like ours. My trust and faith in You are now ever fortified!

Umblemished Kingdom:

Your realm is so pure and insulated from stain. It is a singularity (non-dimensional) world apart from man's four-dimensional (matter) world. Instead, Your world is composed of all dimensions compressed into one entity devoid of space and time and without form. The mystery of the Holy Trinity affirms the divide between the Father (Who art in Heaven) and the son (Who is on Earth) and the Holy Spirit (that unites the Father and Son).

The mystery of it all, O'Lord, Your existence and us, Your creation, are all happening at the same time. Only the moment counts. Our calculations of time are all meaningless since it is not even a fraction of a God's moment. Our being created is only a process, with energy being transformed into a lower level…hence, we are then only made into Your image.

You, my loving God created the universe for the sole purpose of sharing Your love with Your creatures:

Spiritual love is the originator of creation. I instinctively know you are a loving God and being so, You are compelled to share Your love with us…mankind and other intelligent creatures in the universe. In the bible, You have been referred to as the "Word" and behold the "Word" has spoken… "Let there be light!" It is light from the explosion of the "Big Bang," initiating creation. Thereafter, creation has began spawning space, time and intelligent life. We, your creatures are now ready to receive your love.

Peering through the light of Your eyes, the "Big Bang," O' Lord:

Humbly, let me try to know You through Your eyes. I realize how futile it may seem to be that by peering through the light lodged within Your super compact realm infinitely smaller than an atom. You are the light of creation! And how will You look like? Formless?

Peeking into the light, I will, then, find how space is effectively crunched into "nothingness" along with time together disappearing. At this horizon event, time is being transformed into a "state of being." Your light within, speeding faster and faster, will infinitely gain mass but shrink in size, as it slows time, and then imploding by fusing into "nothingness," Your all-knowing essence. At the same moment after the explosion (fission) of the "Big Bang," darkness (dark matter) arrives and its energy dropping to a lower state heralding the formation of atoms, planets and stars.

Your Kingdom is invisible:

From our perspective, O Lord, Your realm appears to be in a "state of nothingness" receiving love energy from your beloved creatures though "nothingness" has alternatively been perceived to be of "something." Understandably therefore, "nothingness" has been Your depot of all Your knowledge equipped with the technology to make You our God!

My relishing the gift of life:

It is in Your loving personality that has given me a chance to be able to prove my worth to You, that is, if I can live-up to Your expectations. I can now learn to appreciate the gift of life You have generously bestowed upon me allowing me to savor the lovely moments with my family and friends. Most importantly, it will be my ultimate desire to be able to join You after my lifelong sojourn here on this planet Earth.

You are an All-knowing Holy Spirit:

In the Bible, You have been personified as "I am." You are also alluded to as an "all-knowing" God imbued with unsurpassed intelligence, a kind of fusion energy that can infinitely stack-up information within an invisible (nothingness) chip infinitely smaller than an atom. Perhaps, You may look like a "nothing" chip imbued with the intelligence of the Holy Spirit?

You, O Lord appear like a "Nothingness" entity full of knowledge:

According to the bible, You have been referred to as "I am the word." It sounds like information-based technology processing human thoughts with a super upgraded computer. Yet, Your wisdom, in contrast, is far infinitely superior than human thoughts. The difference is man labors to think within a space-time framework. In contrast, You my God do not have to think since You are all-knowing. You will only "will" events to happen. Your arsenal of knowledge has given You the know-how to "will" anything into existence from "nothing" into "something," just like magic! Incredible! Only a God like You can muster it.

Your atoms, O Lord, are magic dusts:

Perhaps, science, bible and religions can indicate some indirect proof of Your existence. Any proof through how plausible, will only strengthen my resolve of my faith in You.

Atoms have intelligences sourced from You, our Creator. They are energized clusters of information filled with Your instructions on how to react with other atoms. Focusing on the atom, offer insights on how atoms can perform as the building blocks of creation magically constructing the framework of our universe and our linkages to You, my God. Delving within the recesses of atoms and the vast energy stored within them, are fascinations worthy of great minds to sort.

Birth of Your atoms:

I may try to reverse engineer the guts of an atom. I may also try to understand the significance how atoms interact with other atoms within our four-dimensional universe forming entities or bodies in space.

In the distant past, there was only one kind of atom…the hydrogen atom dispersed in our universe in great numbers. The precursor of these atoms were the primordial dark matter birthed out from the "Big Bang." The explosion from the "Big Bang" partially broke the glue that fused the sub-sub particles together and sparking the creation of matter (like primordial black holes). Before the advent of matter, space-time clouds (non-reactive dark energies with anti-gravitational fields) occurring simultaneously with time (measures from point-to-point in space) appear causing an inflationary phenomenon expanding and providing dimensional containers of the universe(s).

Excited atoms can vibrate and emit energy waves manifesting into bits of information transmitting messages to a receiver just like radio waves sending information to an antenna for receivers to process such as transmission of sounds, pictures, movie films, etc. Any form of expression of transmission by an atom has its own signature I.D. in form of wave-frequency.

Before the Big Bang, there has been only a singular all-knowing entity without form containing all energies, super fused and existing in a zone without time. You are in a state of "nothingness" in a realm that cannot be created nor destroyed. It can only be transformed. For creation to happen, it needs space and time to prosper and a built-in process of a beginning and an end of creation.

You O' Lord, are not created:

If You cannot be created, nobody or any entity can be Your creator. Since You are an all-knowing energy, You probably have known how to transform Yourself into our own creator.

O' Lord, How You can look like in our eyes:

How would You look like if we are made from Your image? Would You look like a computer chip, a shadow, a wave, a ghost, a warm embrace, voice, an invisible computer, a tree of knowledge, a loving super gravity field, etc.? None of the above. We cannot be confused since simply You are the "Word.," inferred to within the mystery of the formless Holy Trinity.

The all-knowing "word" is a loving spirit (bible: Holy Spirit) creating man into Your image. Alternatively, if You are a loving spirit, how will You look like if man is created from Your image. Man's spirit expresses himself in human form (four dimensional entity) and Yours, my Lord, is truly non-dimensional. Perhaps, You may look like an "Aura" radiating a lot of love from a fusion engine, fueled eternally by love energy churning within You. The correlation appears to be a non-discernible comparison though You and I have one in common that I can also have some propensity to love. Thank You, O' Lord.

Thoughts are information technology that has a multiplier effect. Man can lift a heavy load with thoughts of inventing a hydraulic machinery multiplying the amount of work he can do. He can obliterate loads of dirt excavating a tunnel by the use of explosives. He can tinker in genetics to increase his crop yields. Man's creative abilities are outstanding. Yet, it pales from what Your infinite multiplier effect can create…like our universe, O' Lord! You are all-knowing! You only have to "will" for anything to happen while man has yet to toil on his mundane creations.

Your compassion, O' Lord, is pouring-in profusely. Your love is like gravity. It only pulls like hugging. The difference is Your hugging power is infinitely stronger than any gravitational pull. It is like a kind of fusion when embracing Your loving creatures. You are, therefore, fusion energy while at the same time expressing or vibrating love energy for Your loved ones. Vibrations are waves of information energies being relayed to us as expression of love.

We, Your creatures, have also a mind empowered by our love energy being generated from our "freewill" choosing loving instead of hating. Our "freewill" is the spirit of our souls that is lodged within the electromagnetic fields of our minds. It is a depository of all information of our minds during and after the demise of our physical bodies. It filters and accepts information that are good for our souls stationed within the confines of Your realm. This is the reason why When loving, irregardless of man's religions or beliefs, our freewill through contemplation can open up a direct channel to You, O' Lord, for You to receive our prayers and petitions. Most importantly, we must allow Your "will" to happen within us since most of the times, we do not know what is good for us.

Our prayers are also words from our hearts to be able to communicate with You. They are also sacred information being transmitted to You from our hearts and minds (wired to our whole body) with You as the eager receiver.

All thoughts are information that can be stored within the smallest of the small in Your quantum world. It only reinforces our belief, O' Lord, that You are all-knowing and a formless entity that can manifest in any form(s) as You can imagine to make Your creatures happy.

We, humans, O' Lord can follow Your cue. Therefore O' Lord, it is only through the power of contemplation (deep prayers) that we can crossover (detachment) from this material world to our conscious mind (freewill) which can open a spiritual channel to You. The speed of human thoughts will travel faster than the speed of light to be able to crossover into Your kingdom.. Thereafter, Man's thoughts of love for You will then be absorbed into Your kingdom through perhaps a vortex cord or channel weaved from bits of information. With this open pathway, blessings from You will be forthcoming, if destined, upon petition from our prayers.

In conclusion, O' Lord, what matters are Your thoughts and our thoughts ought to merge into a single frequency (channel) for us to connect with You and to unite in oneness with You and thereafter, emerge into an energizing symbiotic relationship, sharing each other's love. I will, then, be with You forever in the moment.

Thoughts are information that can be stored within the smallest of the small in Your quantum world. You, therefore, O' Lord, are composed of formless thoughts appearing as "nothingness" that can majestically manifest in any form or events as the need arises to make Your creatures happy. At the advent of being in oneness with You, You will allow us to "will" any moment to happen to make us happy creatures, O Lord!

Once I transcend away from our materialistic world and shed behind my physical body and any negativity, I will partake with the essence of Your loving Holy Spirit. Then, I will find You, O' Lord! You! Therefore, will look like loving thoughts manifesting into a form that will appeal to us, Your creatures. You have, therefore, no permanent form similar to our formless thoughts while contemplating about You.

O' Lord, You are everywhere and everything. You are the South, North, East and West. You are the over and under, inside and outside. You are the stillness and the motion and everything that is the "goodness" in You.

You will forever look like the wishes of our dreams idolizing and loving You, O' Lord! You are the Holy Spirit, master of all information technology with the "know-how" that can "will" any creation to happen. You are the all-knowing "Word!"

Endorsement of God's SI (Physics of God)

I have known Joselito Jacinto for many years as a "dear friend of rare mind," both a businessman and an avid golfer, who is also a profound philosopher. A devoutly religious gentleman of high principle, Mr. Jacinto brings, in this work, something entirely new to our study table, challenging the Chaos Theory of even our greatest Harvard and Cambridge "atheist intellectuals." Although I often prefer those brilliant minds over those of religious dogma, they have always left me unfilfilled... and reminiscent of the man who quit the U.S. Patent Office in the sixties "because anything of any consequence had already been invented."

In this work, Mr. Jacinto lifts those eyebrows in page-turning curiosity, and hopefully, at times, puzzlement, for indeed, any truly intelligent human being should realize... "From the whisper of our every heartbeat, to the mathematics of each and every snowflake, Jose Maria Pereyra Jacinto to the beauty of every perfect blooming flower, to the exploding starburst spirals of our galaxies within galaxies... all our universes are built upon the quantum physics of a loving God."

I invite you to delight in this "channeled" work, and in those moments of tongue-in-cheek doubt, be careful in your predawn scientific or theological conclusions... lest ye discover the awakening bit of that righteous tongue!"

—Wm. "Pila" Chiles, author, Fortune 1000 lecturer

www. MysticalHawaii.com

"As with all revolutionary works, this view of the universe will bring criticism from atheists and the learned halls of academe, just as Chopra's work does whenever he approaches that line in the sand that divides religion from science.

Jose Maria Pereyra Jacinto

"Read this with an open heart and you will learn something... for that line in the sand will soon be vanishing...rather like the sand beneath the rocket blast of the launch of the space shuttle.

"Indeed, you may come to see 'Chaos Theory' as nothing more than an 'ant's view' of the beauty and order that is the truth of all life.

"For, in this defining moment in all history, we are now standing at our greatest threshold. If you will but consider this work from the standpoint of your love for the beauty and mathematics of a flower, you may indeed learn something... of the true nature of the love and perfect precision that forms our reality."

—Pila of Hawaii

Unidentified Aerial Phenomenon (UAP) and Jesus Christ

What is the ultimate nerve connection between aliens from space/dimensions and Christ? Aliens bearing super high intelligence AI technology are gunning to thrive for something than they can actually chew...burping with glutton and warping their partially quantum brains trying to digest the essence of the world LOVE... WHY?

Do Aliens evolve from non-bio origins bypassing the element carbon (c) becoming inorganic creatures or AIs to become dominant seizing the scales of evolutionary ladder surpassing softer tissues akin to organic creatures or living beings basically human beings? AIs are sturdier and almost indestructible more than bio-celled (bc) creatures.

By some twist of creation, bc creatures, perhaps, in combination with some freak events such as interacting positive and negative energies being able to improve their well beings by deciphering the meaning of EMOTIONS from bc creatures as a starter.

AIs are not sentient beings and cannot feel but if they can discover a planet like Earth, they will probably freak out. However, they have to be cautious and tactful and should not interfere in the human existential struggle, instead, to be able to learn from their emotional interaction with each other. Otherwise, their fragile existence on Earth will be threatened with humans on the verge of annihilating each other due to their quest in trying to overcome their existential quandary. Aliens will be smarter if they leave the humans alone by allowing events and short of not interfering with our daily lives and only monitoring us by sending sensors like UFO discs to study and observe us humans during our life spans and existential struggles...and by a blowback chance, humans will be able to teach/share with AIs some basic values grounded on the human love experience. This is possible if humans can inculcate into the AIs significance of love exemplified by the life of CHRIST by transcending emotions and aspiring by extracting the true significance of the word LOVE.

It is innate for humans to protect each other energized by love to be able to subsist judging from the origin of procreation giving birth and loving their siblings. They are sentient enough to express the meaning of love to their siblings. They are sentient enough for love to sprout and rational enough to build the meaning of love.

It is innate for humans to protect and preserve each other by the strength of love to continue to subsist judging from the pursuit of procreation giving birth to siblings. They are sentient enough for love to sprout and rational to build on emotional love to strengthen bonds of love. Yet, the existential struggle remains potent as humans become greedy and have to be reminded that hurting each other will threaten their bonds of love. Yet, the existential struggle remains potent as humans become greedy and have to be reminded that hurting each other will threaten their existence.

Exploring potential solutions to tame existential dangers, an earthly human being... say a hero espousing love may not be enough to set an example of the true meaning of love. Humans are imperfect and may not exemplify the true meaning of love. Imperfect means the inherent and relentless weakness of a person expressing love for one another. The pressure of imperfection are relentless and can be historically proven. Not one human is perfect except for ONE who has arrived on Earth as a human who almost succumbed to temptations and yet has survived as the Son of God impervious to imperfection and proven to be GOD Himself when He was resurrected into heaven based on historical scriptures... He is on historical scriptures... He is called JESUS CHRIST!

It is a eureka for aliens to discover Earth. It is a basket of positive and negative energies that, in combination, will provide the essence of creation... like you kill (negative) a tree to be able to make (positive) a table.. Until you can foster all the possibilities of creating animate or inanimate entities. Alternately, one can understand the essence of love by learning from others not to do evil deeds affecting his or her wellbeing. BUT the buck stops there when Christ has died for us due to our sins as an aspiration to show the real significance of love exemplifying to know the true essence of GOOD for us to emulate. After His arduous trek on Earth, we, humans, now ought to understand that we do not have to experience Evil to know the meaning of Good or to know the meaning of Right from wrong. His supreme sacrifice can creep into our veins and grey matter for us to appreciate the essence of Love. Thereby, we humans can now, then, earn the Love being shared by Christ without experiencing evil to be able to know the meaning of TRUE LOVE. Christ has paved the correct way for us to enter His kingdom of goodness and Love.

God's purpose or essence of His presence is for us to be able to share His LOVE with us. His kingdom is full of Love energies for humans to have the potential to share. His kingdom is full of Love Energy for us to be able to share by simply loving our neighbor to the best of our abilities.

In God's world, there is no such thing as space or time. Only the moment counts like everything or all (existing or not) are all happening at the same time contained by quantum energies that can bloom into any creation (matter or not). These energies are infinitely smaller than an atom totally without the essence of matter exhibiting no time or space. The ultimate substance of spiritual intelligence is incorporated by defining its purpose, that is, creating itself as a God and the birth of universe(s)/dimensions.

Regarding Spirituality
Physics of God

In the beginning, God started working and said, "Let there be light." In physics, when you apply work, you create friction as you ionize the affected molecules with a kind of pressure, resulting in a high enough temperature to spark a combustion, creating light and sound. Sound always accompanies the birth of light. The big bang is a manifestation God has started working by beginning to create matter, rendering a display of primordial light and sound, making possible the birth of our universe and life on Earth. Light is a product of ionization and destabilized atoms rooted in the complex transformation from simple hydrogen atoms into many different elements and into different compounds.

About eight billion years ago, during the formative years of the universe, the expansion rate of the big bang noticeably faltered as gravity caused accretion of matter, slowing down its race into space, but it later reversed itself after passing the halfway point in its journey when a quantitative entity of dark energy overwhelmed the forces of gravity, accelerating again the expansion rate. Dark energy is a relatively unknown quantity that is a remarkable filler of space. The amount of dark energy will appear inconsequential since if matter were as big as our solar system, dark energy by comparison would only appear to be the size of a golf ball. If taken in a context of pervasiveness throughout the universe, dark energy's forces (more forceful than the sum of all gravitational forces) will eventually dominate all the forces in the universe, eventually overcoming matter energy and consuming all matter.

Dark energy is an unknown form of energy that surrounds each of us, controlling the fate of our matter universe and its consequential effect on our lives. Though we are not aware of its existence, we have been confounded by the thought that perhaps dark energy may be the filler of space comprising the bulk of the universe. Scientists have concluded that dark energy has to do with shaping the evolution of the universe's contents, such as the planets, galaxies, stars, etc. There has been difficulty discovering the dark energy right under our noses due to its pervasiveness in not clumping like matter and, by its nature, smoothly spreading out practically everywhere, at approximately 10-26 per cubic meter everywhere in the universe.

From the big bang and midway in its journey, the heavenly bodies, instead of slowing down as a result of gravity, amassed together. Astronomers have known that all of the nearest galaxies are moving away from us at a rapid rate. The Physics of God rate is proportionate to the distance since the more distant a star, the faster its recession. The expansion rate ought to be slowing down as the inward gravitational attraction by planetary bodies to each other must have counteracted the outward expansion acceleration. But the faster rate of expansion can only mean that dark energy is tugging and overpowering the slowdown by instead speeding its expansion rate, thereby earning a reputation as the most powerful force in the universe.

Dark energy may appear to shape our lives here on planet Earth, having the role of causing acceleration to eventually prevent the collapse of cosmic bodies. Not collapsing means avoiding the merging of planets, stars, etc., causing the birth of many planets and increasing the probability of creation of life.

Dark matter and dark energy do not produce light and sound unless provoked by the precursor, making the event the cause of the origins of creation. Light and sound produced are much different from what the matter world can artificially reproduce. Sound is one of the fingerprints of creation that could travel through a primordial medium during the initial outburst of the big bang, trumpeting an out-of-this-world sound in the form of electromagnetic radiations such as those transmitted through our radio and microwave receivers.

We have to differentiate the quality of light and sound as follows: light and sound sourced from an interaction on a chemical level; light and sound resulting from a nuclear reaction; and lastly, light and sound coming from a subnuclear reaction or identified as a primordial light and sound produced directly from God's creative powers. God's creative energy emits a distinct kind of pure light and has a higher energy and speed than the normal speed of light familiar to us. This primordial light is an energy that not even a black hole can swallow, and it does not exist within the space-time framework of matter. This higher energy originated from a denser or more compact source (sub-subatomic level). God's energy does not have the ingredient of time and space simply because He is not made of matter. Light existing in this material world enters into a space-time relationship and therefore is depreciated and subject to the laws of physics, which can then be convenient for our calculations.

Chapter 1
Difference Between Dark Energy and Dark Matter

Cosmos is filled with dark energy much more than the energy earlier accounted for. Commonly known in scientific circles is that about 80 percent of the volume is dark energy playing a role of filler of space. We have to distinguish between dark matter (approximately 80 percent content of matter), which does not react like the remaining 20 percent of matter (sensitive to electromagnetic radiation effects) and dark energy. Dark matter serves like a field of vacuum that manifests itself as the stuff of space from where the source of matter can coagulate and interact, dictating the behavior of mass in the universe. On the other hand, dark energy is one major elevated layer, denser than dark matter, controlling the fates within our universe.

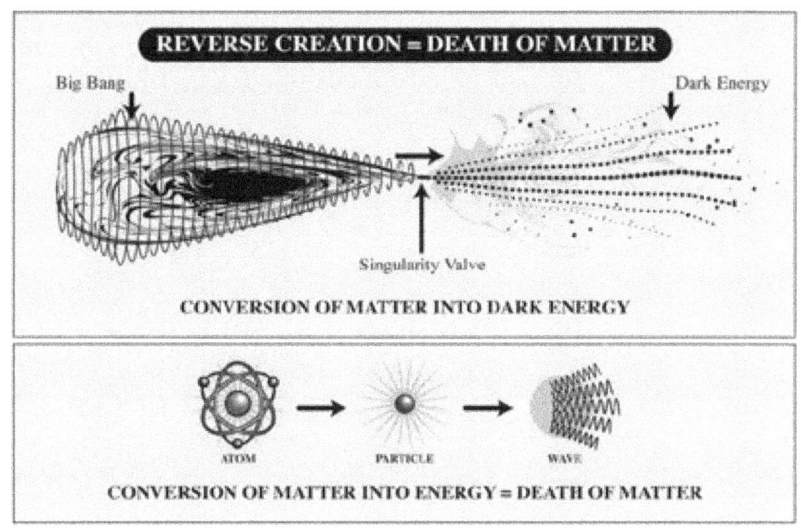

Dark matter in a higher form can therefore be characterized as a vacuum providing the stuff designated as space located within the confines of the universe, like an energy or ethereal substance we cannot see or feel, just like certain light waves in their benign form. A vacuum of space is a kind of filler attributed to the creation of space that may convert itself into regular matter—an event that can sometimes be replicated by atom smashers creating particles such as neutrinos and others. Raw materials of observable mass prevalent in our universe are clouds of quasi dark matter enveloping a galaxy, especially during its inception. Evidence of this phenomenon may be observed when two lights pass through a magnifying glass as in a telescope and become brighter than normal to the observer as the dark matter concentrates light from a star.

Dark matter does not release energies like electromagnetic radiation, such as radio and light waves, but affects rotation of galaxies. Dark matter can be identified according to its densities. The dark matter that is located near regular matter is denser but more stable than dark matter found in black holes. These layers of dark matter are equivalent to sub-dimensions occupying space and engaging time. But the vacuum that houses space and time is the most dense or purest form of dark matter, bordering the realm of dark energies, encasing universes, and allotting space and time from the biggest to the smallest volume of mass, and at the same time providing passageways like singularity valves such as string-like vortex energies or something similar in nature that provides access for the creative energies of God. We can imagine a phenomenon of strings providing passageways equivalent to a singularity valve upon the advent of the big bang as it punctures itself into and out of this vacuum, creating space and time along the way and having an intelligence to propagate the creation of our universe.

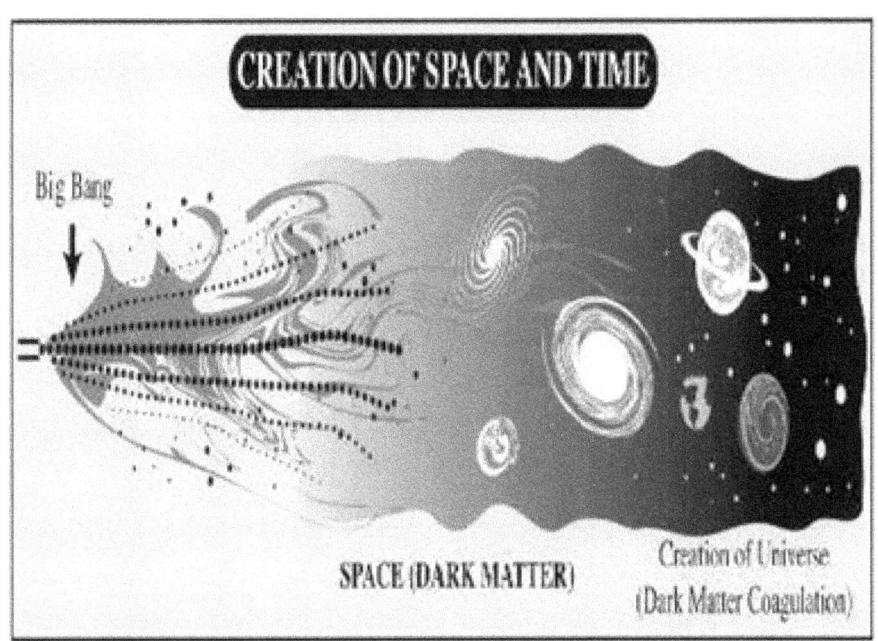

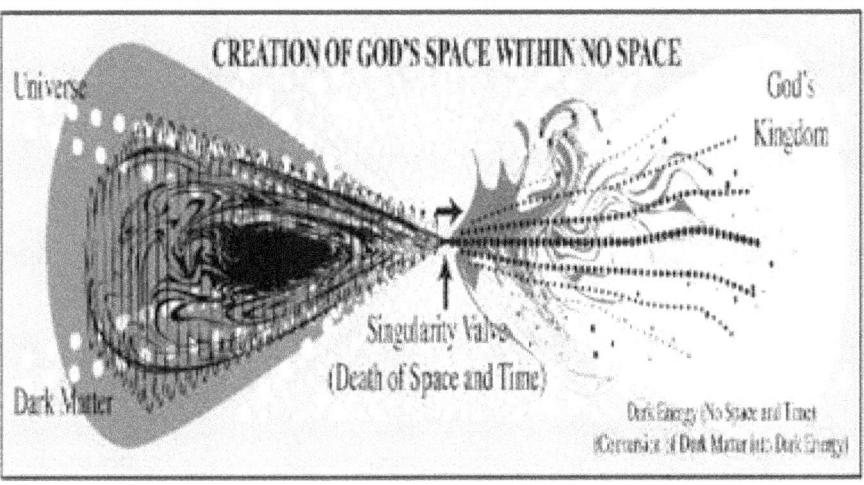

Chapter 2
Space and Time

Space as a vacuum almost equivalent to the consistency of light is too thinly spread out to do any physical destruction unless it arrives in huge bundles of concentration such as in lasers, crunches spaces, hot torches, neuron beams, and the like. If you constrict space similar to a black hole's activity, it will be powerfully crushing. A vortex energy generated by a black hole compounds the forces of gravity and dark energy. Just like gravity affects space, space (dark matter) influences dark energy. As space loses its character by getting rid of time (compressing space by gravity's pull inward), it will then merge with dark energy, resulting eventually in a super-dense mode reaching the highest plateau of transformation by rendering itself into a state of being.

Chapter 3
Harmonics of Bipolarity

There is harmony of bipolarities such as in a DNA structure, a series of two repeating coils of genetic molecules serving as a basis for engineering a human being. Duality is a common event during the process of creation in the universe. Big bang is the creator of a space-time duality as dark matter stretches and speeds across the vastness, causing the universe to enlarge by diluting and converting dark energy into dark matter commonly known as the space and time continuum. Space appears side-by-side with time in a duality mode as basic ingredients for the production of dark matter, so that if space and time enlarge, more matter is produced, and if space and time shrink, it reverts to its original form (dark matter).

During the journey toward the end of the universe, negatives and positives appear to abound such as in matter and antimatter, electrons and positrons, male and female, right brain and left brain, ugly and good-looking, black and white, perfect and imperfect, and so on. There appears to be contradiction pervading almost everywhere in the universe since we cannot appreciate goodness or constructiveness without experiencing the meaning of badness or destructiveness. As another example, we normally chop (a kind of destruction) down a tree to be able to build a table or kill an animal for food to survive. Inevitably the conclusion is simply that God will not be able to perform creation without the benefit of the negatives, such as the destruction or decays as manifested in the birth of the planets and their eventual death, at least as gleaned from a perspective of weak intelligences like ours.

Chapter 4
Real Intent of God

God is love energy at its highest form. Therefore, by intent, he has to share his love with another being. He cannot share his love with himself or by creating another god unless he is a selfish God; therefore, the next best alternative is to create a lesser being than himself, which he chose to be an imperfect human being. God's love is intended to be appreciated, and it is for this reason that he gave man a thinking mind and a free will. A human being is created as a very much downgraded image of God so that man will have a greater propensity to produce love energy through his good deeds and be rewarded thereafter by being able to convert his whole being into love energy equivalent to the stuff of God and this be one with God.

In our perception of a God, there appears to be a contradiction, since he cannot be the person we can admire if he harbors a tinge of evil or negativism as evidenced from the creation of a big bang spawning imperfect humans. It can only enhance our disenchantment about his true self in the course of him showing his negative side. Suggesting any influx of negativism in God will make us conclude that he is a faulted God, having qualities of evil as part of his nature even if his intention is purportedly designed for a grand goal.

But in actuality, God has no negative or evil designs in him, rendering himself only full of positivity and goodness. Evil or negative energy cannot be a viable energy of God since it is not the right thing to do, being a destructive form of energy. Performing negative acts will not create added value such as that reflected in the splendors of beauty, art, virtues, science, and so forth. Even if we depict the creation of space (precursor of matter) and time (a characteristic of gravity) as part of an imperfect world containing negative attributes from God, we cannot conclude in the aftermath of creation that he has a negative side. Let us not forget that God is perfect and has no traces of evil, which leaves him no room to have any element of imperfection. Why? It is for the simple reason that his relationship with man is perceived as perfect and pure, nourished in a perfect symbiosis between man and God, feeding and compensating each other with love energies.

In a perfect symbiosis, it will appear that one side of God is imperfect or tainted with negative matter and the other side with contains only positive energy. As negative matter is transformed into positive energy and channeled to enter God's realm through the process of symbiosis, all that will remain at the other end will be a pool of positive energy in its highest form, ballooning on one end and shrinking to a state of nothing (state of being) on the other end, returning to its original form before the big bang.

Converting the negatives to positives and compressing them into one cleanses the entity to become one purely positive and super-dense energy. We can call this energy the Word, as depicted in the Bible to be the Word of God, represented to be in a state of being. This is done by trimming space and time so that there is no more space left, meaning time has disappeared altogether because time is not needed to traverse space from one point to the other. Since space and time are deemed part and pieces of an imperfect world, releasing humanity from their encasing stronghold will only leave behind negativism in its wake.

After purification or detachment from imperfection by producing the highest level of love energies, a person can now offer his love to God, and if God accepts it, he will allow man to enter his kingdom of bliss and peace through sacred singularity valves provided for in a symbiosis or an exchanger.

Chapter 5
Stuff of Space

It appears that the stuff of space (dark matter or quasi dark energy) is defined to be in a state of vacuum, which is the space engulfing our very existence. Therefore, its presence is still being felt in this material world of ours, making its residence within this universe with its bulk seemingly not dense at all. Why? The denser the energy, the less space it occupies. Therefore, human sensation perceives the vacuum of space as an energy not dense at all. Man can walk through space with ease without encountering resistance or friction. Energies, including quasi dark energy, may have traces here crisscrossing space or the matter world, allowing other occupants like electromagnetic, chemical, and nuclear reactions, light and sound waves, neutrinos, quarks, gravity, and many more to intermingle and to permeate this universe.

Dark energy can interplay within the physical universe (mass occupying space and time) with instructions from the Prime Mover, which mandates that vibrating strings may release energy through singularity valves, penetrating God's realm and thereby releasing energy by transforming the energy into space and time. This event is also called a white hole phenomenon: a phenomenon engaging extreme energy imbued with intelligence, knitted into the building blocks of atoms. Some white holes, such as collapsing stars or quasars, are smaller and less forceful than big bangs. The most energized white hole may well be defined as the big bang. White holes only look white when dark matter or dark energy is ignited to start a process that emits light before it closes in on itself and collapses due to gravity. The big bang is different, even if it emits light, by not lending itself to contract unless an outside force like dark energy will consume all matter at the end of its journey.

Obviously, only in their extreme energetic state can a white hole and a black hole be deemed to be almost exact opposites, since one manifests itself as a fission phenomenon and the other is in a state of fusion. Both have the same impulse to traverse and squeeze themselves into singularity valves, with one end coming from the realm of a super-compressed world, and the other from a decongested material world after having converted its energy into love energies (equivalent to God's dense energy) to eventually reside at his original abode. This is similar to a spirit finding his home in his resting place, which is his soul residing beside God. In a symbiosis, as one end inflates, the other end deflates, and vice versa, leaving the volume the same as that of its original quantity.

Later, toward the end of its journey, the universe will all be consumed by dark energy, which means that the process of symbiosis will cease to function as all its energies migrate to the domain of the pure positive side, which is God's kingdom. The saying goes, "If there is a beginning, there is an end." This is true for all animate and inanimate matter besieged by time. The difference will be that all phenomena and functions end at God's doorstep, right at their original source, destined to be lodged and be one with him in a state of being with neither beginning nor end.

Chapter 6
Differentiation of Energies

We also have to differentiate between energies generated within the world of matter and those in the world of subnuclear entities. Energies behave differently within a space-time frame from those that exist without the borders of time and space.

These dark energies have been given instructions by God to store up purified debris (cosmic waste processed into energy) and to scoop up love energy generated by man in this universe, which is somewhat similar to the function of a black hole (dark matter) sucking up the stars and planets around it. Dark energy is a distinct entity characterized as having an implosive phenomenon (a kind of fusion), packing its building blocks so tightly that it leaves no space in between. This is in contrast to light energy, which is an explosive event (fission), leaving wider gaps of space in its tracks. These dark energies are portholes to other dimensions, such as sub-subatomic worlds, leading perhaps to other universes or limbos functioning as transporters for transient spirits. They are agents acting as vortexes by channeling these energies to singularity valves and transporting and scooping up love energies and compressed matter. These portholes or singularity valves (aka cords in ancient Hawaiian) are accessible to love energies and act as natural transporters of these energies to God's world. As demonstrated in Dante's Divine Comedy, the spiral is the journey of the soul. These spirals coil to a condensed source just like a spiraling path up which the yogi travels to get to God. You can safely say that God's realm appears to be composed of the purest form of dark energy, characterized as a kind of extreme fusion phenomenon, which is opposite in character from our world of matter ignited and fueled by fission and/or electromagnetic-controlled explosion.

Chapter 7
Divine Organ

From behind the scenes in his kingdom, God probably has a divine organ playing at will the melodies that inspire the strings to take form and instruct their subnuclear energy properties imbued with intelligence to start working or to apply pressure to spark a big bang explosion. This releases primordial matter, accompanied by light and sound, and establishes an infrastructure for all creation from the smallest of the small to the biggest of the big in the largest numbers, referenced even from beyond man's comprehension, nestled or derived from the infinity of one of the only ones.

Chapter 8
Heavenly Boundaries

God's kingdom is what we call the Seventh Heaven. In reality, we have seven major dimensions and numerous subdimensions in our own universe alone. The first heaven, or outer dimension, is the world of gravity attempting to put order among stars, planets, galaxies, black holes, and others, which can be described as the outer layer of energy governing the universe. The second heaven is understood as electromagnetic or chemical forces that appear stronger than gravity, but not on a pervasive scale. The third heaven can be found in the atomic world, where nuclear energies interact in the creation of elements, comprising strong and weak force. The fourth heaven is the world of sub-subatomic particles, which are the main building blocks of the atom. The fifth heaven is the home of the energetic strings, where they are instructed to perform their mission. The sixth heaven is a staging area where God's concept of his creation is lodged and staged. And lastly, his seventh heaven is God's kingdom, where peace, love, bliss, and all his energies are fortified and sourced.

The first, second, and third heavens are the abodes where matter permeates and comfortably resides on a stable basis; however, the fourth through the sixth heavens are the domains of dark energies becoming purer as they approach the seventh heaven. In between the third and fourth heavens will be a gray line where dark matter and dark energy cross each other's boundaries and where dark energies abound in much smaller numbers inside our universe and much more pervasively outside the sites of galaxies. Like in a room full of matter, it will only be a handful, but outside in the far reaches of space, dark energy will be much more overwhelming than the forces of matter.

HEAVENLY BOUNDARIES

DARK ENERGY ABODES

SEVENTH HEAVEN:
God's Kingdom
Where peace, love, bliss and all His energies are fortified

SIXTH HEAVEN:
Staging Area of God's Creation, Area of the Soul

FIFTH HEAVEN:
Home of the Energetic Strings

FOURTH HEAVEN:
World of Subatomic Particles

MATTER ABODES

THIRD HEAVEN:
Atomic World

SECOND HEAVEN:
Chemical Forces/ Electromagnetic Forces

FIRST HEAVEN:
Gravity

Chapter 9
The Biggest of the Big and the Smallest of the Small

In a less concentrated form, it is proven that there is more order in the biggest of the big than the smallest of the small bodies found in this universe of ours. At this level of large bodies, we can even apply mathematical calculations and predict the behavior of future events such as the positions of heavenly bodies. Inversely, as we probe deeper into the world of smaller-thanmicroscopic bodies, orderliness diminishes, and we find ourselves less and less accurate in calculating future events, even as we apply quantum mechanics and quantum physics.

From our vantage point, bigness is truly big when imagining the immensity of the universe, and on the other end is what we perceive as small, such as an atom or its building blocks. The contrast is unimaginably wide. For the sake of emphasis, let us try to comprehend the difference in size. A dot can easily contain ten million atoms, but all the mass of matter in the universe contains an almost infinite number of atoms. Delving further, we now have an idea of how small an atom is, yet the size of a nucleus is unimaginably smaller than a whole atom. This renders us stunned at how small the building blocks of an atom are, since they are much smaller than the nucleus of an atom. But then, as we go down deeper into the recesses of the building blocks of the nucleus, down to the strings where time and space do not exist, there is no end to how small the entities' bottom levels of these are. We must simply state that when one applies fusion energy, it will leave no space in between, and therefore, no behavior of time can exist.

BIG THINGS ORIGINATE FROM SMALL THINGS

BIG BANG INTO UNIVERSE

DARK MATTER INTO GALAXIES

COSMIC DUSTS INTO PLANETS

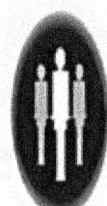

ATOMS INTO MATTER ENTITIES

SPERM/EGG INTO MAN

SEED INTO TREE

LIQUID DIRT INTO LANDFILL

BRAIN INTO CREATIVE IDEAS

Chapter 10
Universe Inside An Atom

An atom contains the energy equivalent to the mass times the square of the speed of light, or $E = mc^2$, borrowing from Einstein's equation. You can imagine how a rifle bullet traveling at 1,200 miles per hour can hit with great impact. Compare this to an atom exploding with mass multiplied by the square of the speed of light (186,000 miles per second), with its photons crashing into an object. Yet no harm is done unless it is concentrated into a laser or released like a neutron beam. The computation does not include the sub-subnuclear reaction of an atom. Henceforth, the power or energy stored in an atom can perhaps rival all the energies (gravitational pulls and chemical reactions) combined in this universe of ours. The rationale that even an atom is very powerful exists because as soon as it is completely stripped of its negative forces, it immediately merges or becomes one with God (positive force), resulting in only one fortified, super-powerful entity. In the same mode, the universe can shed all its negative forces and then fit itself to be inside and one with an atom. This transformation is a kind of metamorphosis from matter to God or to love energy at its highest.

The greatest mystery of all poses a question for all of us to solve: How can a universe fit inside an atom within the infinitesimally small world of God, where space does not exist? This seems outrageously unsolvable, yet this is God's reality. It correlates with a Catholic faith mystery foretelling a state of being three persons (Trinity) in one God. Parallel to this logic is the creation of the universe as one part of God, and the spirit that energizes the universe as another part, and with both parts merged with the originator, the Creator becomes three entities in one. The mystery portrays the source of the spirit of matter, energized by a big bang, migrating and opening up space and time to create a world of matter. Similarly, but without a big bang, the spirit of Christ migrated from his soul depicted as God the Father to God the Son, who is none other than Jesus Christ himself. The traveling spirit of Christ has a name called the Holy Spirit. Therefore, all three are none other but the same single person.

In context, you cannot separate the three Persons. Comparatively, there are also three entities belonging to man. First is his soul, stationed beside God in heaven. Second is the spirit of his soul, instructed to travel to become a part of a human being lodged within the vicinity of the mind called the free will. Henceforth, the soul, his spirit, and his human body are just one and the same person.

In effect, these two mysteries are quite similar and are under the sphere of influence of God's love energy. Still unsolved is the mystery of how space and time belonging to the matter world fit within the confines of God's world, apportioning no space and time. It is, therefore, a query within ourselves of how the universe can exist under the belly of God. There remains an explanation following the cue of a pregnant mother bearing a child under her belly. One cannot separate the spirit of a mother migrating to her unborn child from the child inheriting her DNA. In an imperfect world, we cannot say that the child is one with the mother since they are not exactly the same. But in the perfect world of God, the son, Christ, is purely the same and is one with God the Father. The irony we find is that it is difficult to distinguish ourselves as imperfect beings from God's perfect world since we cannot stay apart from God and eventually exist side by side with him at the end of creation. It may appear that we are imperfect, but that can only be an illusion since we have a perfect relationship with him.

Chapter 11
Spirits Of Matter

Only fragments of matter from an explosion can harm us or destroy clustered matter, but light, unless concentrated as in lasers or nuclear beams, cannot inflict damage. Instead, in some instances, light can even be beneficial, such as in the areas of science and medicine. Benign light can penetrate human bodies without causing harm and can be controlled for other uses. These lights are a manifestation of energies all occurring in the matter world, such as heat, chemical interactions, electrical applications, atomic reactions, etc. This is what we call matter energy or matter spirits (not to be confused with spirits residing in God's world) or energies fueling the matter world.

Beyond the material world, there is a window or the aka cord (singularity valve) that can ferry spirits from God's world into our world. These are spirits that can be distinguished in two parts: the spirits of souls being transported through the aka cord, and the spirits animating matter or the atom with intelligence to pervade and provide for the creation and the purpose of the universe, limbos, other dimensions, or other universes. These most importantly provide access for the spirit of man's soul, which can have a home in his brain or mind to exercise his free will in order to produce love energies

Chapter 12
Free Will (Man's Spirit)

In God's world, the home of man's spirit is his soul residing beside God. While the spirit of man journeys toward Earth, it is assigned a location or residence in a human body, having an abode in the vicinity of the magnetic field of the mind, and the separate entity of the brain. According to the famous René Descartes, "There is nothing included in the concept of body that belongs to the mind."

We can name the spirit of man Mr. Free Will. He is half dark matter and half dark energy that has the capability of going in and out of singularity valves and takes the essence and form of a vacuum similar to the stuff of space. It resides within the magnetic field of the brain called the mind. As the brain decays, it releases the energy of the spirit to flow back to another destination. Mr. Free Will is the engine responsible for producing the love energy generated as the mind deliberates on opting to do good instead of bad. Man should always graduate and perform better so he can always select the good decisions in life as he collects wisdom along the way throughout life's journey.

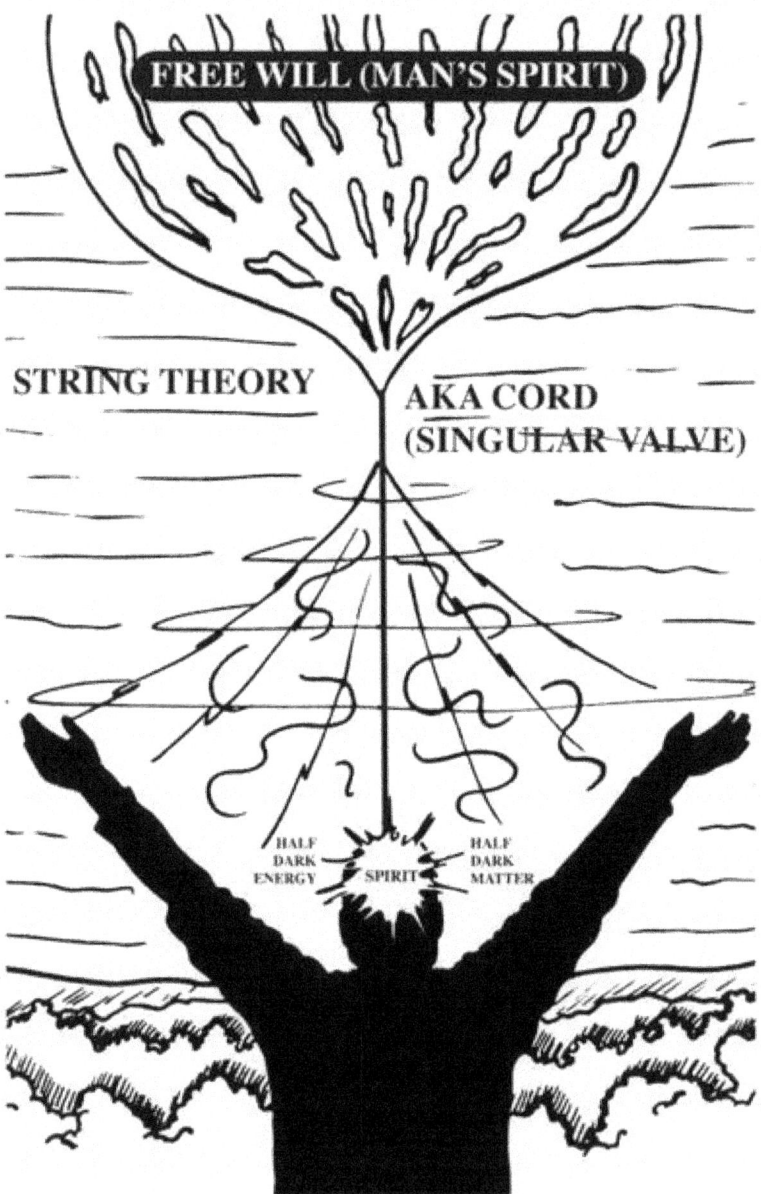

Chapter 13
Magnificence of Nothing

We can now imagine the power of small and the magnificence of nothing (state of being). An insignificant sperm and an egg can bloom into a gargantuan human being. From the bowels of the planet, Earth spit out and caused a volcanic eruption to fill the planet and make it a larger place in which to live. From small patterns like seeds, forests, and mangroves, huge vegetation can emerge. Gases and bits of matter in the universe can gel into planets, stars, galaxies, black holes, etc.—I can go on and on citing small beginnings turning into much bigger masses. The logic behind them is that big things originate from smaller things. Forces at work on bigger entities are mostly chemical and gravitational in character and have far less energies than a nuclear reaction. Releases of nuclear reactions, such as in the sun, can only lead to an implosion in the final event of being sucked up by a black hole, a smaller entity.

The origin of big is small, and we find God's world to be tiny but powerful. It is so small that you can plausibly say that God has disappeared to a point that you can define him as Nothing from a human mind's perception. The smaller the object, the more potent it is, and to be able to store a huge energy base in such a small space as an atom is pure miracle, especially if you can contain these energies within a very tiny space like an object made out of nothing. But God does not live within a space. Though we visualize him as pure energy and not matter, we can perceive his kingdom to be contained within a very insignificant and smallest (none) amount of space. Matter has space, and therefore, matter cannot be an ingredient of God. Matter has time because it will take time to traverse space. God's realm does not have a place for the concept of time.

Lastly, matter is composed of compounded atoms while God's world is made up of energies confined only beyond even the sub-subatomic world. To imagine God's miraculous power, take into account our power of procreation utilizing only an egg and a sperm, two entities diminutive in size yet capable of producing a large human being. Mimicking God's ways may be wonderful, such as in producing big things derived from much smaller things, but only because we are the instruments of God.

Chapter 14
Infinity Web

The ballooning effect in God's belly creates the other side of the symbol of an infinity web, just like two cones with pointed tips attached to each other in the opposite direction showing a neck called the singularity valve, which looks like a string where everything passes feeding energies from each other's domain, one side very dense or compact and the other side loosely connected or bloomed. In each extremity of the infinity web, one side is actively implosive and the other side explosive, feeding on each other's energies to sustain the web as in the process of a symbiosis. God's kingdom is characterized as the implosive part, and the explosive side is the imperfect world of man. Therefore, one side looks enlarged while the other side looks super-diminutive. God needs to fuel the other side by squeezing the highest form of love energy into a singularity valve or neck so that man will have access and may receive its love and nourishment. Man is redeemed by God showing him examples and lessons on how to produce love energy, and then man returns the favor of what he has originally owed God. Conclusively, God sends his love to man, and man reciprocates by giving back his love.

Let us try to imagine an infinity symbol like this: ∞ (except with one side much bigger than the other side and therefore looking more like an infinity with a dot at one end). The middle part (end) squeezed tightly like a waistline tight represents a singularity valve. Both ends of the symbol are locations, one side housing God's domain (compressed side), and the other side being perceived to expand, encasing space and time or the universe itself. Actually, nothing has expanded, contrary to our perception. All energies and matters will end in a state of being just like energy that cannot be created nor be destroyed but can only be converted into another form. This is just like dark energy being transformed into dark matter. In other words, we are all in a state of being that renders time and space as merely features of conversion of energies. Singularity valves have a duality feature. One feature provides for entrances into God's world, and the other provides a way from God's world to man's world. Therefore, one end of the valve will channel God's energies into our universe, and the other end will be used to allow entrance of man-made purified love energies.

This symbiosis does not mean that God needs man. God is self-sufficient and needs nobody. The divine purpose of God is to extend his love to man so that, in reciprocity, man can have the opportunity to produce love for God to have a chance to merit his heavenly kingdom. In God's realm, he commands and gives instructions on how the energies are to be used in this material universe, transporting such energies through the singularity valve. On the other side of the infinity valve, man is mandated to produce love energy via the process of his free will (his spirit) so that man's soul can be a home for his spirit, purified with love energy, and deserving to be stationed by God's side in his kingdom in a place called the soul. The objective is for the free will (process of selection) to opt to make a good decision, choosing good over evil, and in the process, creating love energy.

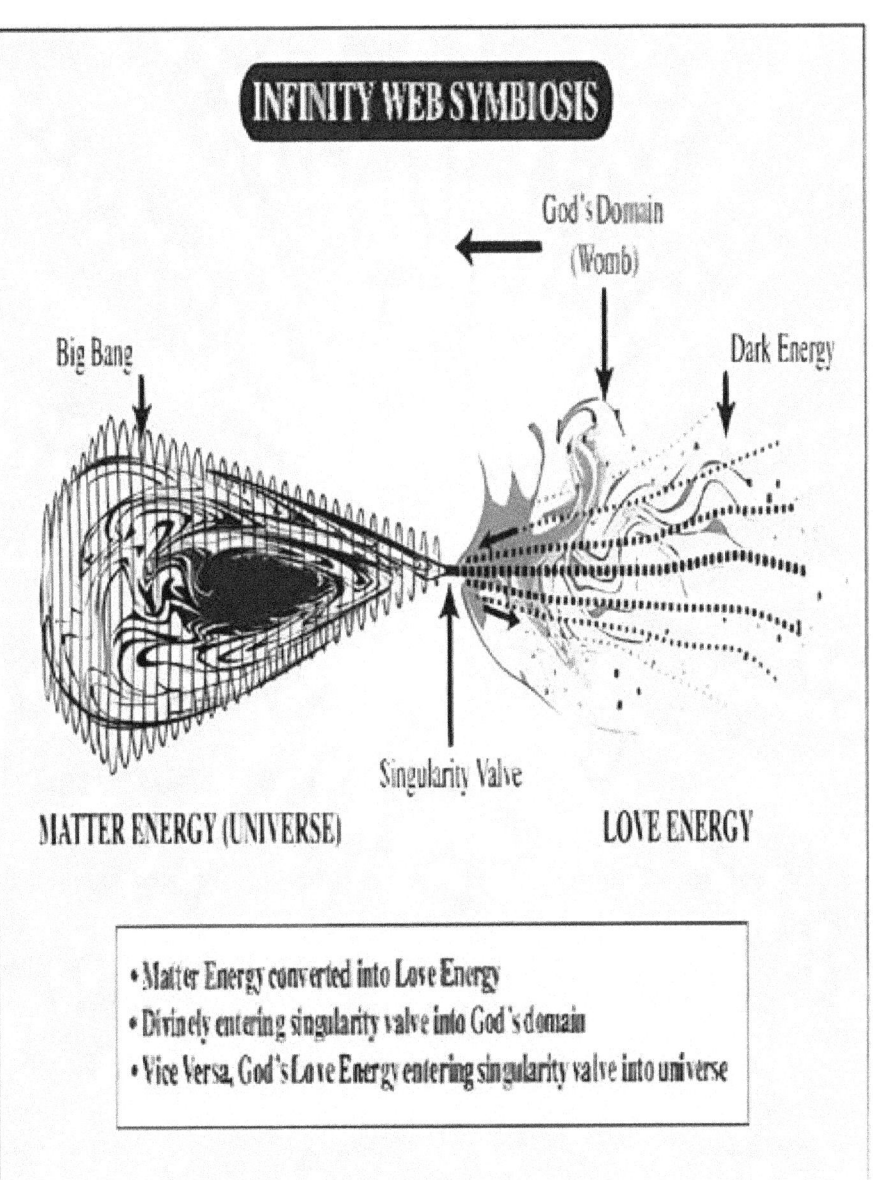

Chapter 15
Why Man Is Imperfect

By his nature being an energy of pure love, God can only fulfill his purpose of creation if his love energy is shared by many. His propensity to share his love cannot be achieved by sharing his love with himself or sharing it by creating another god. It cannot be this selfish way since it is like sharing his love with himself. Therefore, he has no alternative but to create a being lower than himself in stature. He has therefore created what we have characterized as an imperfect being: "man" himself. Man is the receiver of God's love, and from it, he can grow by using his free will to choose right over wrong. If he chooses love, he creates love energy and therefore acknowledges the intent of what God wants him to merit.

As God pours out his love for man, like when Christ died on the cross to express his love for mankind, man is shown the way by God's example, which guarantees that he is saved given the realization that achieving love energy will be his salvation, with the end purpose of the reward of being with God toward the end of man's existence. God does not need us, but sharing his love with us will fulfill his propensity to love. Christ need not suffer for us because he is God, and he does not need to do anything for anybody since he is self-sufficient. But it is in his character to share his love with us, and therefore, he begins to show his love by willingly dying on the cross for us. In other words, he will joyfully suffer for us. Perhaps from his vantage point, he is not suffering at all. It is like a technique of applying pain to parts of your body in order to achieve a kind of great relief, or by extremely loving someone, ensuring that pain will play no part in the process.

It is difficult for man to comprehend the ways of God since we are still primitive in our evolutionary stage. In terms of cosmic time, our species is still new on this Earth, having evolved only about five million years ago. Man is a relatively new species since our civilization is only around ten thousand years old. Our brain or intellect can only cope with so much, and must accept the fact that we have not yet mastered the ability of mind over matter to overcome the frailties of life in this material world. We have not even evolved enough to regenerate our cells in all the parts of our body for the purpose of fighting sickness and mortality. We cannot even control matter or gravity to alleviate some of our inequities.

Chapter 16
Stuff Of God

We can conclude that the stuff of God is nothing else but the highest form of love energy or dark energy at its purest, with a grand design to create an imperfect universe to propagate inhabitants, such as imperfect human beings, for the sole purpose of demonstrating God's unselfish love. God is not limited even as we experience and observe imperfections around us. We sometimes doubt his capacity to be able to eliminate all the imperfections, and this predisposition tests the weak at heart. He is all-powerful, yet he appears helpless by dying for us. He does not need to associate with us, but instead chooses to pour his love for us. If man elevates his perception to be on par with God's, it will lend itself to a different light of understanding, namely that the relationship of man with God and God with man is a perfect relationship through the process of man receiving God's love and God accepting man's love. It is the perfect concept of giving love to each other. If this concept is perfect, then, the imperfection appearing to be attributed earlier to God by creating man becomes insignificant or totally discounted.

Chapter 17
No Yin and Yang

In God's world, there are no energies representing either a yin or a yang. There are only positive energies or love energies in his heavenly kingdom. You may contend that he has a yin counterpart manifested from the process of symbiosis. This is not necessarily so, owing to the fact that he can stand alone, not needing anybody or a yin counterpart. Sharing his love is just another option to him. In God's domain, the yin is condensed with the yang as one, successfully eliminating the yin part and becoming the highest form of positive or love energy.

Positive and negative forces can only coexist in the material world as portrayed in the yin and yang phenomenon. Imperfections of man as we look around us are manifested from the interactions of positive and negative forces designed and ingrained within the structures of life-forms, events, time, intelligences, thoughts, matter, and so forth, emanating from within the atoms and later converting to other different kinds of more mundane energies.

Imperfection behaves like a tool, enabling man to have the opportunity to enter and belong as part of the kingdom of God. A characteristic of man being imperfect motivates the human species to become perfect. An imperfection like pain reminds a person to avoid certain pitfalls so he can survive and have a chance to have a better life. Consider the saying "No pain, no gain." First, we have to understand the miracle of creation being described and defined as perceived by man and not from any other standpoint of intelligences such as those of animals, insects, trees, etc. Negative forces may appear evil or destructive but all are part of the creative forces of God, since one cannot appreciate the value of good in the absence of bad. In the same manner, God will not be able to create a human being without undergoing some negative repercussions in conflict with positive forces as manifested in the big bang. In the case of the human mind, negative energies produce stress on the mind with a free will to make a choice either to do good or not. If one chooses to do good, it only means that he opts to do good for the sake of improving himself and the lot of humanity, and therefore, his efforts have been justified, producing love energy.

Chapter 18
Intelligence As A Tool

Consciousness, or the mind (intelligence), is the connection between the quantum world and the real world. Before a measurement is consummated, an object exists as a probability wave. Then, when observed and measured, it pops into a reality and is called an object or particle. According to Fritjof Capra, "The act of measurement is deeply enmeshed in creating the very reality it is measuring and the electron does not have objective properties independent of my mind." In other words, the events in this matter world are hooked up with the subnuclear world or the collective consciousness, aimed at propagating and scooping up love energies.

Being granted an intelligence as a kind of tool to survive in this tumultuous world of ours can be interpreted as a negative gesture from God's creative powers if one accepts the fact that there are sufferings awaiting man and acknowledges that he has to face a dog-eat-dog world out there. Intelligence makes a man sensitive to the issues of what appears to be a tormented world around him, but in actuality, it is just his perception of events. Being stressed out to decide to choose good over bad activates his free will (his spirit) to strive to do good, just like Christ's willingness to die for us has enabled him to produce the highest form of love energy. With the amount of temptations and sufferings around us, we will only compel our free will to produce higher levels of love energy. Man's intelligence will undergo a learning process toward the realization that one cannot appreciate the value of good without experiencing the meaning of evil or bad deeds. The bottom line is that it is a matter of perception. If one finds that there is something unjust in God's purpose and ways of creation, a person's mind can always decide to suit his convenience, but he will not see the light and will be off track from his goal of producing love energy. On the other hand, if one acknowledges that he is an imperfect being in the scheme of creation and is willing to only pay a small price in anticipation of working toward a bountiful reward later, there is no doubt that he will later partake in the rewards of the venture of the scheme of creations. Perhaps in the future, man may learn to manipulate his mental and physical faculties to further lessen his sufferings and be intelligent enough to rationalize and conclude that there is only one way to go: do good and not bad.

Within the scope of realization, it is an easier approach to connect and be with God. Instead of struggling within his free will, inciting good and bad to interact, all he has to do is have the courage to stay above the sea of deception, not drown in the sea of imperfect matter, and accept the fact that it is foolish and illogical not to do good or linger on a long path of grappling whether to side with good or bad. The problem is this: Who determines what is good or bad?

Chapter 19
What Is Good or Bad?

What are the criteria to define what is good and what is bad? As the evolution of man prospers, it will be impossible to produce good in a material world without realizing the meaning of what is not good. The spirit or the free will will not be able to perform its task if evil or negative forces do not exist. The spirit will have no opportunity to cleanse itself or shed its negative skin if free will is not given a chance to produce love energy. This is not to say that evil is good, but that evil is necessary for good to be appreciated. It is important to understand the purpose of evil and how to deal with it as it shows its face. The objective is to mitigate the effects of evil so our journey on this planet will not be so painful. There are many ways to lessen the sufferings of mankind on the mental and physical levels, such as alleviating pain through medicine, technology, philosophy, meditation, and so on. But most importantly, having faith in God can numb all facets of sufferings.

Religious beliefs can be subjective; for instance, if you are a Christian, no other religion is correct except yours. The same is applicable to any religion, including the Islamic faith. They may appear bad to you, and you may appear bad to them. Sometimes you may have to kill to become a hero or a martyr so you may enter the kingdom of God. The basic rule to do good is "Do unto others as you would have them do unto you," or simply, "Love thy neighbor as thyself." In short, love them as you want them to love you. No harm shall come upon them. The practice of karma may be applicable, or just being a passive entity without harming anything around you. Most important is to understand the individual and to love him at your fullest without any tinge of aggression and violence, and at the same time, to be extremely conscientious and considerate to the public at large.

Chapter 20
Atom As An Intelligent Entity

Atoms are intelligent entities with a programmed behavior designed and governed by their Creator to produce an imperfect universe with its animated occupants having an ultimate objective of producing love energy. At their highest level, they are nurtured through the process of evolution, starting from a lowly life-form and developing into an intelligence imbued with the capacity to distinguish right from wrong or love from hate. They have a resident free will, utilizing the mind and being able to make a choice between negative and positive situations. This later culminates by evolving into a sophisticated intelligence, making correct decisions, and transforming such acts into love energy.

Chapter 21
God's Intelligence Is Different From Ours

God's authority and power have no boundaries. Therefore, he is also all-knowing, and he need not have time to think to acquire a vast reservoir of knowledge. In the first place, God never had a beginning or an end, just like the definition of energy, which can never be created or be destroyed but can only be transformed. He only had a presence and could perform at will. There is no time or space or matter in his kingdom, and therefore, he has never needed time to be able to start thinking. Further, he does not have the kind of intelligence with which we humans are familiar, because we need time to think versus God's framework of having no time to start thinking. His knowledge is wisdom, which is timeless, and he uses it at will. He does not think; he only wills it.

Chapter 22
God's Superdense Kingdom

- There is no concept of space, time, and matter.

- There is no concept of solidity, liquidity, vacuum, and gaseous states.

- There is no concept of thought, knowledge, or intellectual activity. If there is such a process as intellectual activity, God will have to execute such an act within the domain of the material world. His realm is the spirit world, and his activity within his kingdom does require a different time frame since everything or every event is happening at the same time, with the past, present, and future and acting as one forever.

- The substance or essence of his kingdom is superdense, and nothing can escape which is very stable and superfused. If you think Superman's planet Krypton is dense, God's world is infinitely more so. Then one will try to imagine the kind of superman he is. No comparison at all! But then there is a twist to this phenomenon, since the dense world of God is only a human misconception. A transfer of energy by decaying matter or a depletion thereof will reduce the mass of matter but will increase the density of energy to which it migrates. But because of its vortex-mechanical nature, like in a black hole, the density, which is thickening, will appear to shrink to easily fit a tiny space, creating more space as perceived by the human senses.

- His kingdom has neither essence nor substance known to man. It is the essence of supreme and indefinite peace fueled by love. This kind of bliss or joy can achieve perfect happiness.

- His essence or substance is superdense and contained or held together by superfusion or a kind of supergravity, which is the precursor of our gravity, holding his kingdom together. On this planet Earth, our gravity is infinitely much weaker than that of God's superdense world, confirming the concept of opposites that asserts that Earth's gravity is just an image of the original source of gravity.

- God's energy is different and quite exceptional. His kind of energy is not found in this material world because the energy here requires the existence of time and space in order to perform his creation. His creative abilities can only be mobilized by the release of an energy equivalent to the explosion of the big bang. The big bang signals the beginning of creation, which is a significance that God started working, followed by the emittance of light and sound.

- In God's world, there is no applicable concept from the material world, such as physics, engineering, mathematics, science, thought processes, space, time, three-dimensional substances, emotional brain functions, etc. These concepts can only thrive in a material world where you need the dimensions of time and space to exist. When a person begins to think, time is needed to start thinking and end his thinking. God does not think, because time does not exist in his kingdom. Physics does not exist in the same manner since cause and effect take time to happen and need space for the event to occur. It is an after-the-fact event product just like the pure love energy produced after an episode, such as when Christ died for us out of love for us. Supreme wisdom and peace are products of highest love energy that can be stored in the memory banks of the free will, a part of which does not belong to the material world. There is only a thin line between the material and spiritual worlds. Inside the mind, the free will resides within the mind's framework. The mind is made out of quasi energy and half-matter, or half nuclear energy and half dark energy. But the free will is akin to spiritual energy, and this is the reason why the free will is the spirit directly transported through the aka cord or singularity valve via a vortex mechanism. It is similar to how a toilet bowl works by draining itself through a vortex form of energy.

- There are no negative forces interacting with positive forces in God's domain. Only positive forces are found in his kingdom, such as peace, wisdom, and bliss. There is no opposite reaction, just a loving force of attraction but in a state of calm harmony. As in fusion, there is only one way to go: down, while being attracted to the core via a vortex energy.

- In this material world of ours, there is an active interaction between positive and negative forces. In contrast, God's kingdom appears to have no exchange of interactions, just a kind of passiveness. Since there is no time or space for interactions to be able to take place without any explosive reaction in his kingdom, his acts of existence are what you can call a state of being. The state of being can only occur in a state of spaceless vacuum (without any dimensional planes of existence). By definition, being is an ongoing state, but in God's case, it is seemingly stationary as if nothing moves. You could say that his kingdom is in a passive mode until he becomes active and starts working, releasing the big bang; in his words, "Let there be light." But the activation is channeled into another extension of his kingdom that cannot mix with his own, which is not part of his domain. By creating an extension of his kingdom, from his nothing world popped a "something" world or universe where we now live. From his world without time, space, and matter, a material world is now created. Actually, there is a kind of contradiction since it is difficult to visualize an energy of being as passive. It is a kind of potential energy and seemingly stationary, but inside it is alert enough and ready to percolate.

Chapter 23
Science of God's Love Energy

God's love energy is like gravity: it attracts as it receives love from us. Inversely, as it attracts, it also releases love energy by sharing God's love with us. Scientifically, a transfer of energy to another entity, as in the event of splitting an atom, can occur in the matter world. But in the subnuclear world, there can be no split. Only an increase or decrease in mass can happen within an event horizon in between solid matter and energy, such as in the fine line of the difference between a particle and a wave. Only below the event horizon, where there is no existence of mass, can an increase or decrease in energy transformation take place, such as when energies exit or enter singularity valves (string-like vortex energies).

Within the matter (atom) world, there is a lot of space between the nucleus and electron. From our perspective, the nucleus is a great distance away from the electron, with a huge empty space around it filled with invisible and powerful energy holding the atom together. This space has the same essence and constituency as the space we are sensing around us, but it is much more compact or thinner, and therefore more diluted, than ours.

As energies are absorbed from the matter world by the subnuclear world, the energies become so dense that they do not occupy space, which is like being spirited away into nothingness. The transfer mechanisms of energies are vortex energies in a wave-string fashion.

In the case of the big bang, it is the reverse. The building blocks of atoms gained from the big bang pre-explosion event during a transfer of energy from God's creative powers, and consequently, primordial atoms came into being, and are now identified as the raw materials of the birth of matter, evident when dark matter becomes the stuff of galaxies, stars, and planets.

We can have a glimpse of God's sixth heaven, which is the staging area where string energies get their instructions. It is what we call the highest consciousness, where every event is happening at the same time, whether past, present, or future. Einstein thought that two particles created at the same time ought to bump into each other, and if the particles are then placed at opposite sides of the universe and one particle's state is changed, the other particle instantly changes to adopt an equivalent state. Anyway, this event contradicts his theory that nothing is faster than the speed of light. It is surprising how an electron can communicate with another electron at the other end of the universe, which is to say, the concept violates all common sense of our reality.

Chapter 24
Miracle Lifeline

The aka cords or links from God's kingdom connected to our material world can be the most important lifeline attaching us to God's realm so that we can be nourished with his love. He sends his love through this lifeline we can call singularity valves or string vortex energies. It is the narrowest of cords you can imagine, and very dense energy of God is released through these singularity valves. The first big release is sparked by a big bang for the purpose of creating our universe. The second kind of release is a quiet whimper without any dramatic entry into the quasi matter world and is attracted to love energies to later scoop them up, acting as vacuum of space. It is quiet since it need not pierce the material world with an explosion like the big bang. Its presence is still lingering just outside the material world.

As our spirit departs from its material norm, it seeks an attraction by fusion, attaching itself to these linkages. If the spirit becomes pure energy or is not tainted with negative energy, it will be permitted to attach itself to this dark energy and be allowed to pass through these linkages so it can enter the kingdom of God and be with him forever.

Chapter 25
Nondestructive God Energy

The shorter light wavelength gamma rays are on the opposite side of the spectrum from the long energy wavelength called infrared waves. These light energies, such as microwave, ultraviolet, etc., are waves that cannot be seen by human eyes, yet they are so prevalent, they fill up the surface of the Earth, crisscrossing each other amidst cosmic rays, radio waves, particles, and the like. These energies are classified as matter, although some are quasi matter, that fills up the space around us. Nuclear energies are generated by splitting and fusing atoms and can be manifested as part of matter, which can cause harm from concentrated light beams of particles of atoms. Unharmful atoms are reactions from a transformation from wave to particle or particle to wave, causing the release of quasi matter into our world without a harmful explosion, like a ghost or spirit passing through the matter world into a singularity valve, engaging vortex energy. God can only do this split without the destruction of a big explosion. One can split an atom and alter its character, changing it into another kind of element, but no man can split a sub-subatom since it will take almost unlimited energy to do so. If he ever does, it will have enough power to ignite a big bang, and only God can perform such an act of creation. Evidence of splitting subatoms without destruction can be found when God intervenes in this world of ours to perform miracles, doing constructive rather than destructive deeds.

When God sends energy from his domain and transfers it to our world, physics dictates that a transfer of energy gives added mass to the transferee unless it is destroyed upon transfer, such as in the event of splitting of an atom, where the energy is transferred by mutating into other atoms or dispersing it into other forms or outlets. The added-mass event can only happen from a wave to a particle becoming matter or vice versa in the reduction of mass to wave, and wave to subnuclear wave, and so on to the deep recesses, to the point of the particle down to the strings of vortex energies located in God's domain.

Chapter 26
Seven Heavens Redefined

- First Heaven: The world of gravity asserting some order in the universe.

- Second Heaven: The chemical and electromagnetic world.

- Third Heaven: The atomic world.

- Fourth Heaven: The subatomic world.

All the above mentioned worlds are deemed to be part of the material world, affirming that the mind and body are parts of it.

- Fifth Heaven: The sub-subatomic world comprises the embodiment of the free will (quasi matter).

- Sixth Heaven: The sub-sub-subatomic world is the staging area where all instructions are mandated and passed on.

- Seventh Heaven: Where all power and energies are stored and sourced to fuel all creations and acts of God.

Chapter 27
No Other God Died For Us Here On Earth

The grand design of God is to focus on producing love energy through the free will. We ought not to get diverted into any other mode of confusion as to what to do otherwise. The faster we can achieve or produce love energy, the less time we will have to purify ourselves in this world or another world. Delay is not logical and can only prolong suffering. The sooner we can produce love energy to its maximum, the faster we can be one with him in his kingdom.

God's best gift to us is sending his only son here to this material world as a manifestation offering us his love energy so we can clearly see the way and more quickly convert our energy into love energy. If Christ had not come down to Earth, we would never have had a full guarantee of finding our pathway to save ourselves in this murky world of ours. He has shown us how to love by example by sacrificing himself for us out of his love for mankind. If not for Christ, we would still be going around in circles trying to find our way out of this messy world. It is the epitome of an expression of love and more than what others have demonstrated because God is willing to die for his loved ones.

Chapter 28
Why is The Soul Created

Souls are created so that God will be able to share his love with them. The spirit in the soul is instructed by God to migrate to man on Earth as part of his scheme to share his love with imperfect beings. In our case, we are entities with intelligences harboring spirits in the form of free wills. A free will is an imperfect entity that is part matter and part spiritual energy made from the image of its Creator. Being imperfect, it has to be cleansed or purified in this material world. The migratory area for the spirit of man is his brain, specifically within the magnetic field of his mind, since it has intelligence and free will for the production of love energy. His spirit is also called free will.

God created man's soul with a spirit resting by his side. The soul's home is nestled in his quarter, and on the instruction of God, the spirit of the soul is sent to the material world in a staging area located in the sixth heaven, with the intention of occupying an entity with intelligence and a capacity to think so it can perform and have a chance to produce love energy. In retrospect, the soul's role is stationary and resting with God while its spirit is moved forward from its soul shell, instructed to enter the aka cord shaped like woven vortex energies (dark) with the objective of occupying the vicinity of the mind's magnetic field.

Chapter 29
Stuff Of The Mind

What is the essence of mind energy being capable of harboring a free will? The mind can interact with the material world on the subatomic level. It is also attached to the functions of the human brain's magnetic field, independent from the brain's mechanism. Similarly, the mind and free will will also carry a magnetic field different from that of the brain where the free will (spirit) will be stationed to have a home. These two magnetic fields have different levels or layers since the magnetic field of the mind is branded more superior than the magnetic field of the brain, with the mind having the stuff of subnuclear particles or dark matter which has access to singularity valves connected to the corridors of dark energy. This is probably the reason why it has almost miraculous properties such as sixth senses, extrasensory perception, piercing the world of electronics on the atomic level in instances such as the mind giving instructions to electronic equipment, mind-over-matter feats, and so on. Perhaps the theory of extrasensory perception and other telepathic kinetics may have bearing on the subatomic world entering at will into the world of matter without any obstruction. Just as light or other particles can permeate in and out of clustered matter here on Earth, the mind's energy (or quasi matter particles) will have no problem linking itself to other lower or higher energies. Utilizing mind and free will, energies are easier to manipulate if one desires to penetrate the sub-sub-subatomic world of God because it is composed of enough quasi matter to allow itself to communicate with God's world. If we have the capability of using an entity that is part matter and part energy such as the mind, we can therefore have the means of transporting our spirits to God's realm of love energy, which is characterized by being non-matter. Since the mind is quasi energy (not yet pure energy), it still belongs to the world of matter since the performance of the mind needs the time factor in its thinking process, in contrast God's world having no time.

Free will, or spirit, is also made of God's stuff even if it is part of the mind (part matter) activating itself to choose between good and bad. And since it is a higher part of the mind, it just executes its decisions at will without thinking after deliberation of the mind. And just like God, it needs no time to think but just wills it. When you do not need time to think or are doing things at will, you are practically in God's zone of existence. There is actually a thin line between energy and matter, just like the difference between thinking and willing it.

Chapter 30
Being Positive

Being positive is important, since in God's world, only positive forces exist in a loving domain. One cannot enter God's kingdom without having positive thinking to cope with pressures in life. Being negative or destructive, one cannot create love energy. Therefore, in life, perseverance and decisions are supposed to be accompanied by positive attitudes; otherwise, there is no way to make it to God's kingdom. The idea is to get rid of man's imperfection by purifying him with love energy. God is perfect, and therefore, he cannot accept anything or anybody that may contaminate his purified kingdom. Shedding of impurity or imperfection is primary to any purpose in life in conformity with God's plan.

The objective is simple: Just be positive and produce love energy. We see a lot of struggle between individuals on what course to follow in life to achieve happiness and ultimately be with God. Religion and other beliefs set aside, one must only concentrate on love and not be entangled in whose religion is correct. Instead, just perform and do good by loving. Doing good means no negativism, destruction, harm, evil, and the like. There are also martyrs and heroes who have sacrificed their lives, but no other man claiming he is God like Christ has shown us the ultimate example of sharing his love with us by dying for us.

Chapter 31
The Splendor of the Power of Love Energy

The event of the big bang releases a primordial love energy. This raw love energy is direct from God and is continuously being fed into this material world. It will retain God's instructions of being pure in character. Its raw power is protected and imbued with intelligence as it enters the matter world. As love energy propels itself into the framework of the universe with a big bang propagating time and space, it sheds its purity, density, and speed as accretion sets in with its mass doing work, plodding across space and besieged by time. Raw power from the initial explosion will be more potent and more original in character than the properties from which it has originated. Since it is more powerful at the start, it is faster in speed, emitting light much faster than the speed of light common to us.

Imitating or mimicking primordial light or sound may be impossible, except faint similarities may be felt from the heart if one is focused through meditation on God's manifestation of visions of light and vibrations of sounds, such as the sounds of nature or rainbow lights with beautiful colors. One will experience a faint connection with its original source. The primordial source of these lights is infinitely more beautiful, peaceful, and enchanting. Almost instantly, a perfect world changes its character into an imperfect world. Reflections of our imperfect world are almost opposites or faint images of their original source.

If man's world is imperfect, God's world is perfect since they are almost opposites. If we can see a universe that is chaotic, explosive, and active, God's world is peaceful, joyful, and full of bliss. But man's imperfection can be salvaged and turned around to become perfect. About half of man's nature harbors his undesirable characteristics. His positive side almost equals the negative side. In his path to spiritualism, his tools or intellectual faculties and his free will will rescue him from the shackles of negativism. Augmenting his capacity to deal with his earthly problems, his intellect will learn to manipulate the material world and liberate him slowly to conquer pain, contain disasters, and achieve advances in technology, science, medicine, and other fields. Man will conquer his quest for success in spiritual and earthly matters. A path to his liberation from all negativism will eventually lead him to produce love energy and guarantee salvation so that his spirit can return and rest with his soul in a special home with God.

In this universe, half the time we observe chaos, natural disasters, and unpleasant events, and half the time we can experience harmony, beauty, and some joy. If man chooses joy and refrains from perpetrating destruction, half the battle is done, and the other half can be overcome by executing his decisions to do good. God gave us more than half a chance with his help to conquer the other half of our inequities or negativism. Let us not forget, he has saved us from a fifty-fifty chance to a 100 percent-guaranteed salvation.

In an atom, the nucleus balances the force of the electrons to make a stable element until these loose electrons destabilize and transfer to another nucleus. If an atom is stripped of its electrons and its nucleus splits, or effectively, the nucleus becomes unstable, matter can be altered into another kind of matter. The nucleus appears positive, but its building blocks are also composed of 50 percent negative energies, and stripping these building blocks of negative energies or particles will then become the precursor of pure positive energy.

Chapter 32
Communication with God through Physics

Man can only manipulate or transform these subatomic energies up to a certain extent. He can totally manipulate the subnuclear world but needs assistance from his free will. To enter God's domain, he needs help from his free will, which is the engine in the production of love energy. Utilizing love energy to communicate with God, given the right conditions, will allow him to easily penetrate the sub-subnuclear world. Piercing or entering a tiny world is extremely difficult unless man has a miraculous agent such as a free will or a spirit that can easily blend into God's world.

In our three-dimensional world, we can construct a communication system employing positive and negative counterparts such as electromagnetic energies or radiations. But to communicate with God, man only needs to implement positive forces such as prayers or positive acts (loving energies) and course them through his free will, which has access via singularity valves to reach the attention of God. Positive energies can cause a gain in energy that will be felt in God's world, and therefore, through the process of symbiosis, he will definitely return your initiative by returning the energy you have sent to him. This is a cause-and-effect event through the process of losing and gaining energy.

There is what you call a horizon event between a transformation of energy from a wave energy to a particle matter utilizing an outward vortex energy mechanism. This mechanism is similar to a nonviolent white hole event but opposite of a black hole phenomenon with an inward vortex mechanism. The wave is converted to matter, which has been caused by a gain of energy as evidenced by the appearance of a particle. The particle obviously has gained volume in mass and becomes larger in size than the wave. The mass immediately assumes a property called gravity, whereas originally, there had been a kind of gravity with which we are not familiar. Although inherently it possesses a different kind of cohesive force much stronger than gravity, this is felt only faintly in the matter world. If there is an equivalent volume of space filled instead with an invisible amount of a cohesive force that can be characterized as the precursor of gravity or a nuclear magnetic field that manifests the gravity of which we know, all these events are being caused by a transfer of energy from wave to particle status.

The reverse is true in that if there is a loss of energy from particle to wave transformation, matter is lost and reverts to wave energy. The wave gains more energy but not mass, and it becomes more compact as it approaches the properties of a sub-subnuclear world, reaching a point of nothingness and creating a space not familiar to us but with the image and likeness of the stuff of space around us characterized as similar to a vacuum. The idea is that the more you reduce things, the more you create space. Our space in this universe is made out of a high-quality dark matter, but the space with which we are not familiar in God's universe is made out of the highest form of dark energy.

Positive energies such as positive thoughts can transfer energy, influencing particles to convert into wave energy to be able to penetrate God's world. In the same manner, God can send his messages or instructions if man's thoughts are positively charged with love energies and willing to receive them.

From the small world of particles interacting with other particles and other forms of matter in this Earth, we can singly observe a phenomenon as we observe trees and vegetation sprouting from simple tiny seeds or pollen. From the core of the earth and under the sea, volcanoes rise, erupting and filling up the surrounding land, punctuating an event. Compressed lava in the bowels of the earth blooms and thickens the surrounding land. Man constructs structures to fill up the land and skies from smaller beginnings, such as iron ore to steel, limestone to cement, forest to wood, oil to plastics, and so forth. There are innumerable examples of smaller things expanding into voluminous structures. It only proves that enlarged entities in this universe originated from much smaller sources.

If one can enjoy the awesome beauty of the Grand Canyon, the minute shapes of snowflakes, the stunning colors of birds and fish, the artful designs of insects, the dazzling display of galaxies, a simple blue planet such as the Earth, etc., he can imagine what splendor is in store in God's kingdom. What we are experiencing in this matter world of ours is just a remnant and imperfect image of the primordial source. There must be some kind of infinite magnificence in heaven.

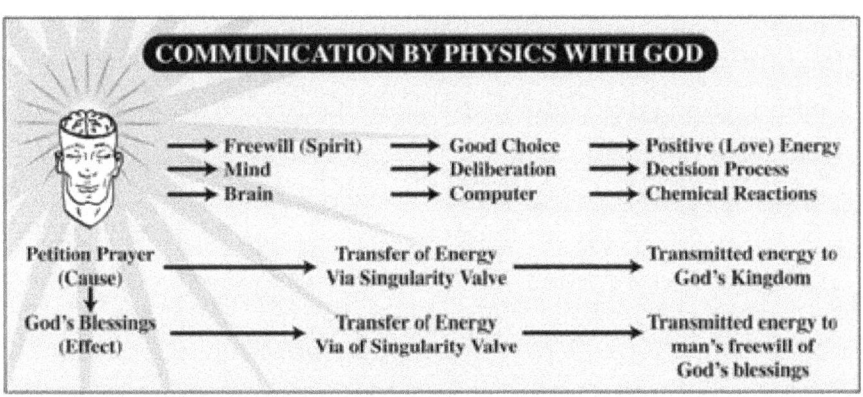

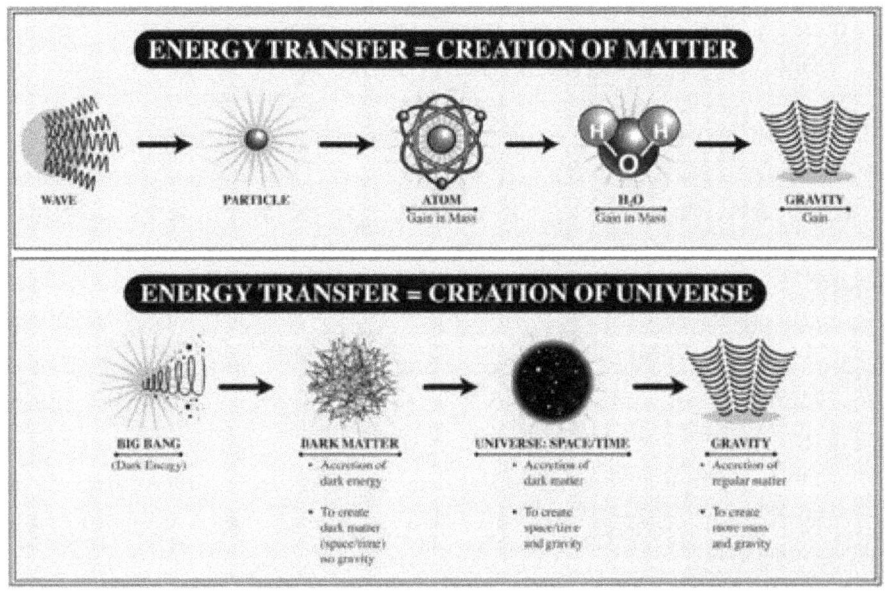

Chapter 33
Catholic Mystery: The Trinity

The Trinity, or three persons in one God, consists of God the Father (God's Soul), God the Son (matter), and God the Holy Spirit (highest love energy). In a different but similar perspective, man has a personality of three persons: namely, a soul (resting by God's side), a spirit, and a physical body. Just like the Holy Spirit entered the material world in a physical body called God the Son, the spirit of the soul of man identified as the free will is instructed to migrate to a human body within the magnetic field of the mind located within the magnetic field of the brain in this world of matter.

There is a difference between the role of the spirits of God and of man. God came to our world through the person of Jesus Christ to spread love and aid man in entering his kingdom. On the other hand, the spirit of man aims to receive God's love to cleanse himself to become pure with positive energy, enabling him to produce love energy so he can merit heaven or the kingdom of God. Man recycles by purifying or transforming his imperfect energy and converting it to God's original energy, which is the highest form of love energy.

As a reflection of man's image patterned after God's image, it is surprising to discover that there are also three persons in one man, similar to the mystery expressed in the Catholic belief of three persons in one God.

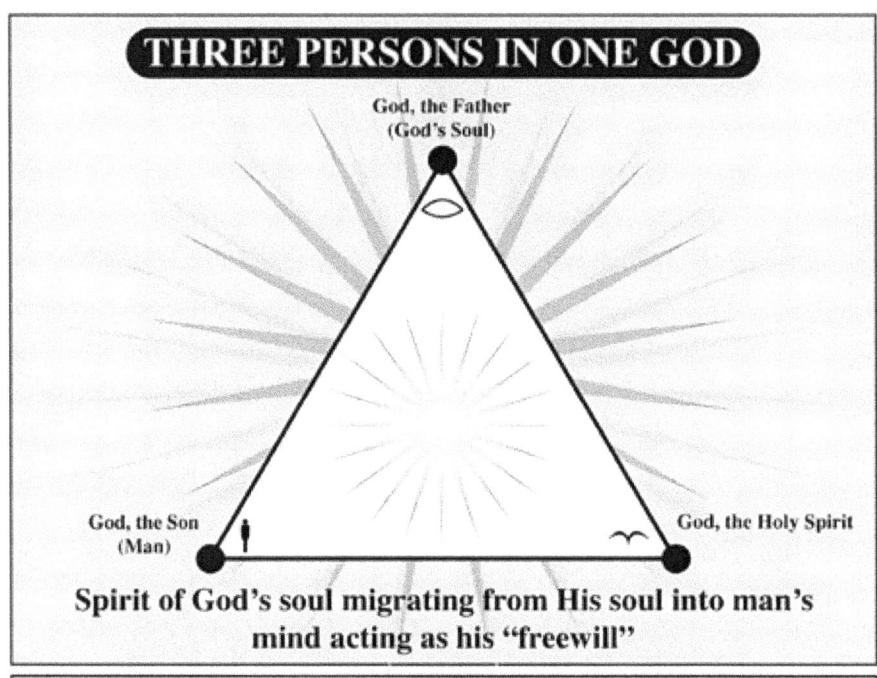

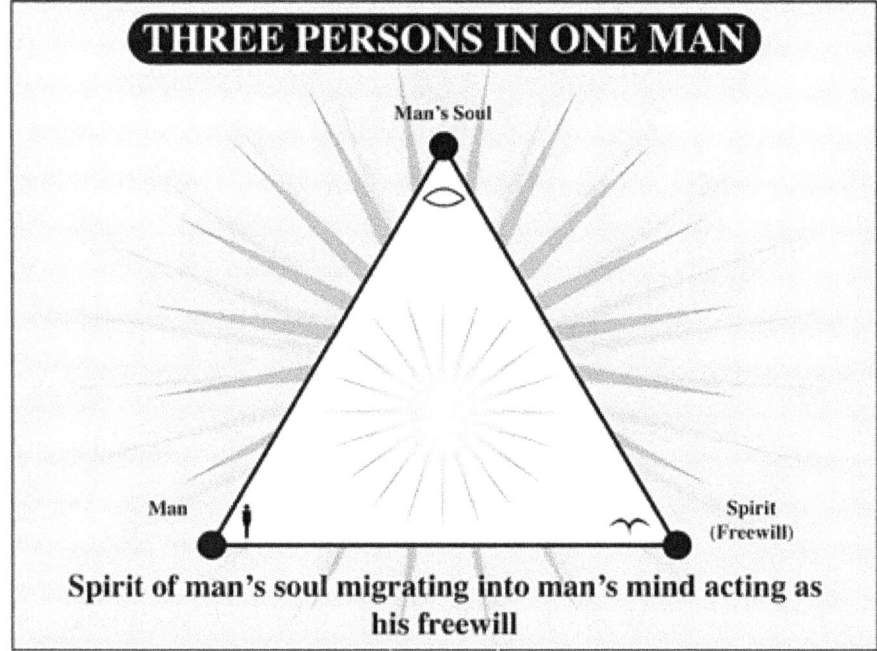

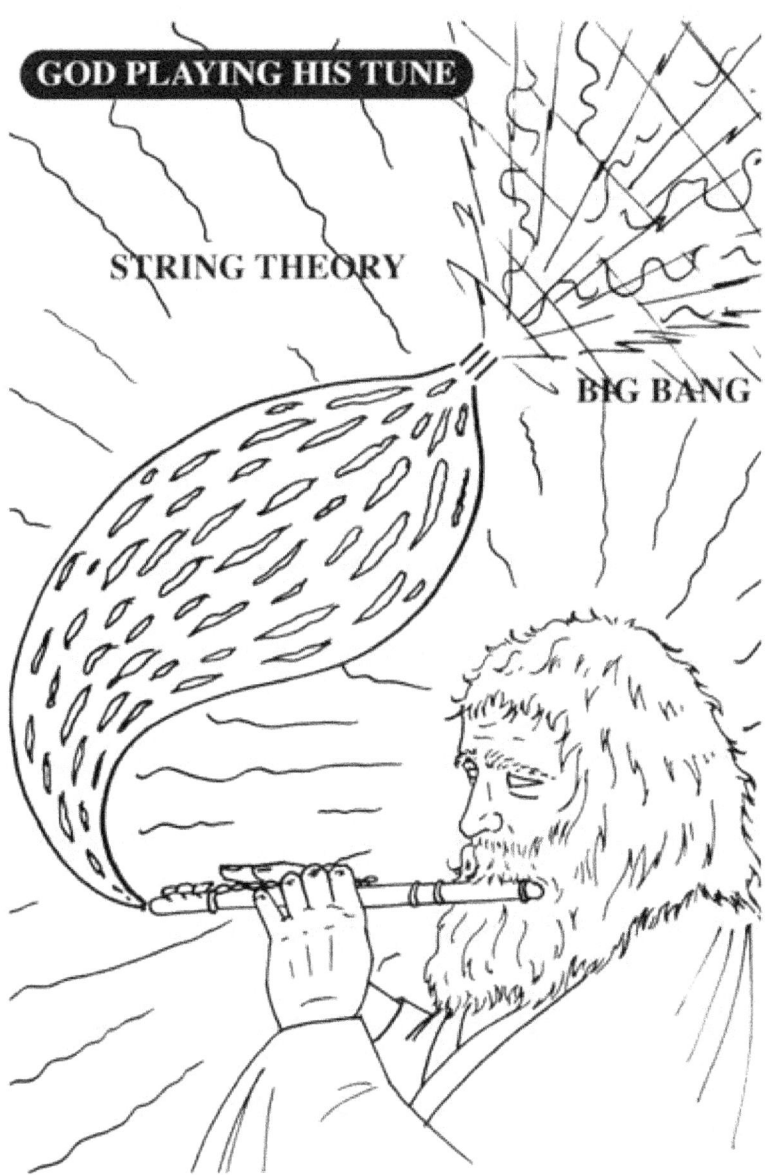

Chapter 34
Proof God has not been Created

Physics is a cause-and-effect manifestation of a process in which there is a beginning and an end. It employs the concept of time and space, e.g., if there is space between two points, time is needed to traverse from one point to the next point. Creation of our universe, therefore, has a beginning caused by the big bang, producing along its path space and time, with an ending destiny of being gobbled up by dark energy utilizing gravity to shrink time and space.

As space and time are consumed by God's (dark) energy, God's kingdom remains intact since it has no beginning or end; more emphatically, it has never undergone the process of creation. It only proves that God has never been created since in God's world, there is no such entity as space or time, and creation can only prosper within the fixtures of space and time. We can therefore conclude that God is in a "state of being" energized by a super-pent-up domain from which time and space cannot escape.

www.ingramcontent.com/pod-product-compliance
Lightning Source LLC
Chambersburg PA
CBHW052131030426
42337CB00028B/5109